Bugs.

4

Where?

Up here.

BUGS!

By Patricia and Fredrick McKissack

Illustrated by Mike Cressy

SCHOLASTIC INC.

New York   Toronto   London   Auckland   Sydney
Mexico City   New Delhi   Hong Kong   Buenos Aires

To MaJon Carwell,
our nephew and happy reader.
—P. and F.M.

To my brothers: Claude (Nick), Kevin, and Scotty,
who occasionally bugged me when we were kids.
—M.C.

Reading Consultants
Linda Cornwell
Coordinator of School Quality and Professional Improvement
(Indiana State Teachers Association)

Katharine A. Kane
Education Consultant
(Retired, San Diego County Office of Education
and San Diego State University)

ISBN 0-516-23890-6

12 11 10 9 8 7   3 4 5 6/0

Printed in the U.S.A.   10

First Scholastic printing, November 2001

One fat red bug.

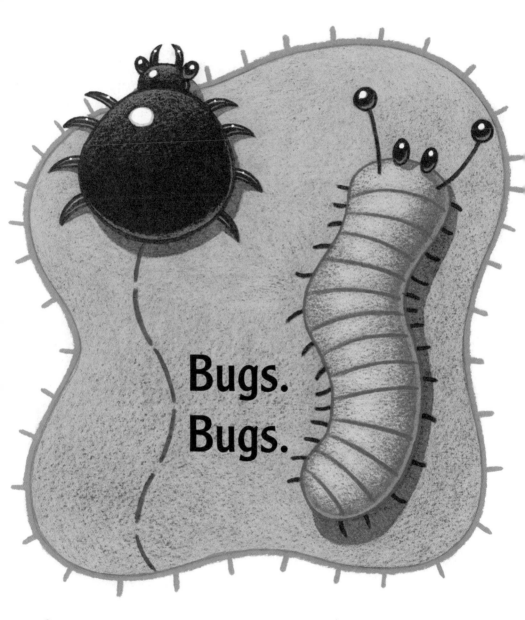

Bugs.
Bugs.

Where?

Under here.

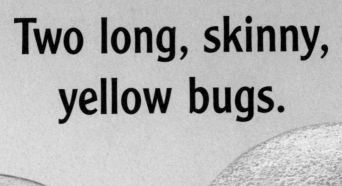

Two long, skinny, yellow bugs.

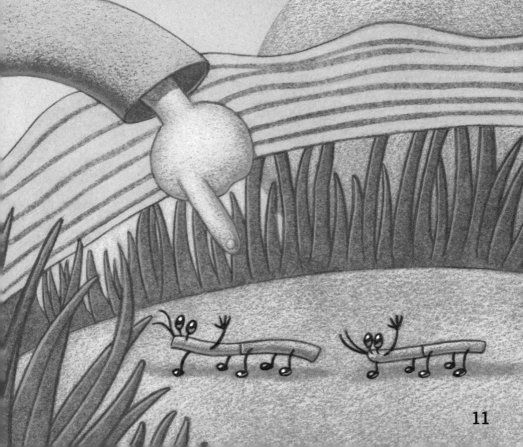

Bugs.

Bugs.

Bugs.

Where?

Over there.

Three fat, green bugs with two big eyes.

Bugs. Bugs. Bugs. Bugs.

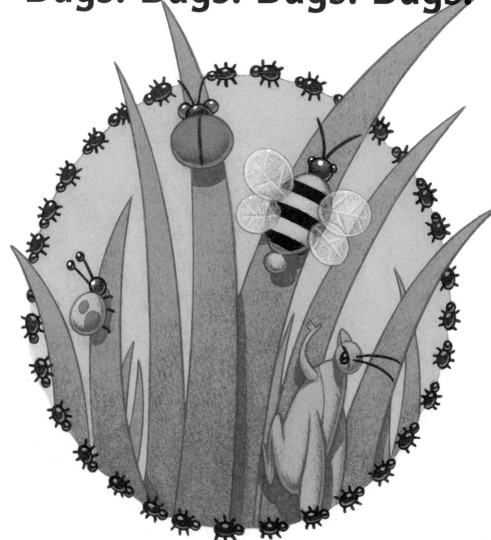

Where?

In here.

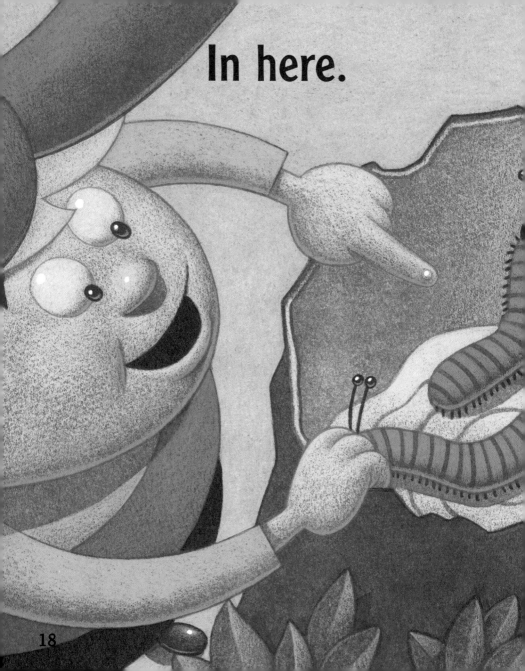

Four bugs with four hundred feet.

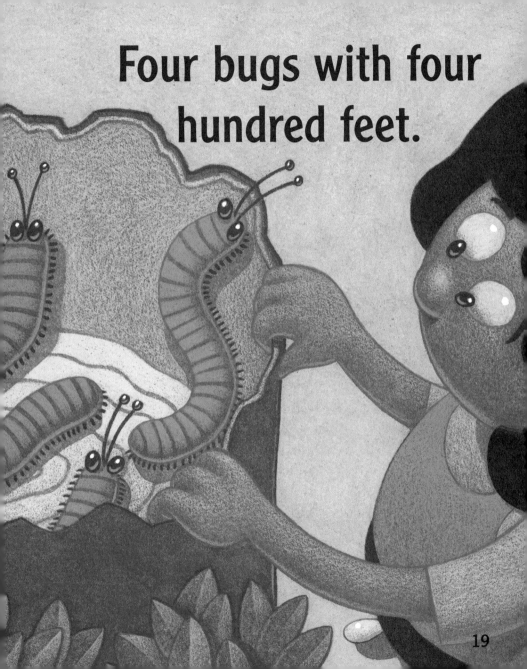

Bugs. Bugs. Bugs. Bugs. Bugs.

Where?

Out there.

Five little bugs that fly here and there.

Bugs. Bugs.

Lots of bugs.

Where?

Where?

Everywhere!